ADVANCEMENT

Understanding the Purpose, Process and Proceeds of Divine Promotion.

Charles Omole

WINNING FAITH
OUTREACH MINISTRIES

London. New York. Boston. Lagos
Published in the United Kingdom.

Cover/Book design by: Lacepoint Publishing
www.lacapoint.ie : email:services@lacepoint.ie

DEDICATION

This book is dedicated to all the children of God, who are yielded tools in the hand of the Master; sent to pray, preach & proclaim His Word until Revival comes. Your manifestation of Advancement is now.

TABLE OF CONTENT

INTRODUCTION

This book will change your live and bring excitement into your spirit. That is a guarantee. We will be looking at a very crucial part of today's societal dynamics.

We live in a media world. With increasing use of new technologies, people are led more by what they see. As the saying implies, the book is sadly always judged by its cover. This unfortunately has influenced the values of many children of God. Many in the Kingdom now seem to judge success purely by external factors. How big your house is. How good your car is. How expensive your clothes are. How big your church is. How many material comforts you have been able to accumulate. These superficialities seem to be the yardstick for success in the Kingdom of God today.

But if the foregoing list is true; then Nebuchadnezzar will be a success in the Kingdom. Pharaoh will be a kingdom celebrity of success. After all, these men had all the external marks of success based on the current conventional thinking. The truth is that advancement, like success is not primarily a physical thing. We need to change our paradigm in the Church and begin to make assessment based on spiritual imperatives rather than physical status. If you meet Joseph when he was sold into slavery; he will not strike you like a successful person. And if you meet him in the prison; you will not give him any fighting chance of becoming significant in life.

Yet the bible says that Joseph, while in prison was a "prosperous man because the Lord was with him". So Joseph must have had something significant that was mostly visible in the spiritual. He clearly was not a physically prosperous man as a prisoner. So as you can see, Advancement in the Kingdom is firstly developing spiritual stature, which will eventually reflect in physical advancement and promotion. In the Kingdom, it is not physical first; it is spiritual first then the physical will follow.

This book explains the purpose, process and proceeds of advancement in the kingdom of God. You will learn how to advance where it matters. You will learn how God uses all your experiences, especially the negative ones; to advance you. You will also learn the keys to advancement and how to grow in stature. Even though your physical status may appear to be declining, you are still advancing; as long as you are growing in stature. You know how a footballer retreats first (move backwards); in order to generate the momentum that will be needed to give force to the ball when he runs forward. So your apparent backward slip was part of the divine game plan. It is called "retreat to advance". It is not over for you by a long shot. You have success locked up on the inside. The world will soon hear from you, if you don't give up.

So be excited as you read this book, and you will be liberated by the word of God. You will come to see advancement as God sees it. You will learn to be content in God for where you are and more importantly, you will learn to appreciate the strength of the spiritual over the physical. This is your secret weapon as a child of God. I am excited for you; welcome to your season. Read, learn and be blessed. God bless you.

Charles Omole
2010

ADVANCEMENT, BUT NOT AS YOU KNOW IT

A dvancement in the Kingdom of God is not the same as the Secular world defines it. This is largely due to the fact that in the Kingdom, Advancement is not so much defined by output, but by the process involved and it measures more of your Stature (Spiritual) and not your Status (Physical) alone. Since the spiritual controls the physical; it is possible to have advanced in the Spirit but your physical situation may not yet reflect it.

The bible says in Genesis 39:23 that Joseph *"was a prosperous man because the Lord was with him"*. The only problem with that statement is that Joseph was in Prison and thus in the physical he did not yet look like what he was in the spiritual. So Joseph had advanced in stature; but his physical circumstance did not yet reflect it. Therefore in the Kingdom of God, Advancement is primarily a Spiritual phenomenon that ultimately controls your physical circumstances. So you advance in the spirit first, then your physical advancement will follow. Anything that exist in the natural that is not a result of a spiritual reality cannot last. That is; you win the battle in the spirit first and then it will manifest in the natural.

The Basic English Dictionary Defines Advancement as follows:
1. *A forward step; an improvement.*
2. *Development; progress*
3. *A promotion, as in rank.*
4. *The act of moving forward.*

Hence as far as the world definition is concerned advancement is a state of continual progress and promotion. The act of moving forward. But in the Kingdom of God, moving backward can be moving forward. I will explain this in more detail as the book progresses.

"When Pharaoh drew near, the Israelites looked up, and behold, the Egyptians were marching after them; and the

Israelites were exceedingly frightened and cried out to the Lord. ¹¹*And they said to Moses, Is it because there are no graves in Egypt that you have taken us away to die in the wilderness? Why have you treated us this way and brought us out of Egypt?*¹²*Did we not tell you in Egypt, Let us alone; let us serve the Egyptians? For it would have been better for us to serve the Egyptians than to die in the wilderness.* ¹³*Moses told the people, Fear not; stand still (firm, confident, undismayed) and see the salvation of the Lord which He will work for you today. For the Egyptians you have seen today you shall never see again.* ¹⁴*The Lord will fight for you, and you shall hold your peace and remain at rest.* **¹⁵The Lord said to Moses, Why do you cry to Me? <u>Tell the people of Israel to go forward!</u>** ¹⁶*Lift up your rod and stretch out your hand over the sea and divide it, and the Israelites shall go on dry ground through the midst of the sea".* **Exodus 14:10-16 (Amplified Bible)**

Exodus 13:3-4 (AMP)

³*And Moses said to the people, [Earnestly] remember this day in which you came out from Egypt, out of the house of bondage and bondmen, for by strength of hand the Lord brought you out from this place; no leavened bread shall be eaten.* ⁴*This day you go forth in the month Abib.*

Exodus 13:4 (Holman Christian Standard Bible)

⁴ *Today, in the month of Abib, you are leaving.*

Exodus 13:17-18

¹⁷*When Pharaoh let the people go,* **God led them not by way of the land of the Philistines, although that <u>was</u> <u>nearer;</u>** *for God said, Lest the people change their purpose when they see war and return to Egypt.* ¹⁸*But God led the people around by way of the wilderness toward the Red Sea. And the Israelites went up marshalled [in ranks] out of the land of Egypt.*

It is God's desire for you to "Go Forward" or experience advancement. God instructed the children of Israel to move forward; so seeking to advance cannot be a bad thing if God commands it. But we need to be careful not to get entangled with the world's definition of advancement; thereby abandoning God when we are being taken through "process". For children of God setbacks can be setups.

BASIC PRINCIPLES OF ADVANCEMENT IN THE KINGDOM OF GOD.

1. **GOING FORWARD REPRESENTS A CONTINUOUS MOVEMENT IN GOD.** There

is always a forward for the children of God. They moved forward out of Egypt; then they were ask to move forward again by the red sea. Each time you will need to go forward to get to the next stage of God's purpose in your life, but not to where it ends. You will still need to go forward again to the next level.

"Ye have compassed this mountain long enough: turn you northward". DEUTERONOMY 2:3 (KING JAMES VERSION)

In God, movement is constant. You have to keep going/moving forward.

2. **IF GOING FORWARD IS EASY FOR EVERYBODY; GOD WILL NOT NEED TO TELL MOSES TO COMMAND THE PEOPLE TO MOVE FORWARD.** Moving forward therefore requires faith and trust in God and not a focus on your enemies.

3. **GOING FORWARD IS WHAT THE ENEMY WILL NOT EXPECT YOU TO DO.** Pharaoh thought he had cornered the Israelites since there was a sea in front of them and the army of Egypt are coming behind. Your enemy expects

you to be cowed and afraid. He will tell you; you are in a strange land and you cannot make it here. You have to show the enemy that God specialises in creating streams in the desserts.

4. **TO BE ENCOURAGED TO MOVE FORWARD INDICATES MOVING FORWARD INVOLVES CHALLENGES AND OPPOSITION GREATER THAN YOURSELF.** But without moving forward; God will not be able to show himself mighty on your behalf.

5. **GOING FORWARD ADVANCES YOU; BUT GLORIFIES GOD.** This is a win-win situation for both you and God.

6. **ADVANCEMENT (GOING FORWARD) IS A PRODUCT OF SUCCESSFUL SPIRITUAL POWER ENCOUNTER.** You have to overcome an opposition to advance; but we know that the weapons of our warfare are not canal…but mighty through God.

7. **YOU WILL NEVER EXPERIENCE NEW HEIGHTS IN GOD; IF YOU DO NOT GO FORWARD.** You will be relegated to the basics of God's provision if you refuse to advance.

8. **AS WE SAW WITH THE CHILDREN OF ISRAEL; MANY TIMES IF WE FAIL TO**

ADVANCE; THE ALTERNATIVE IS NOT BEING STATIONARY; BUT DEATH. If the children of Israel had not gone forward in faith; the Egyptian army would have killed them.

So do not think you have a viable choice to not going forward. In many cases it will be either you advance or you die in your current position.

So if we examine the life of Joseph (Genesis 38-42); we will be able to see vividly the operations of advancement in the Kingdom of God. I want you to look with me as I do a basic Up and Down analysis of Joseph to illustrate this point. So let us do it this way:

1. Joseph was the favourite of his Dad and given a Coat of many colours. THAT IS UP
2. He had two astounding dreams. THAT IS UP
3. He was hated by his brothers. THAT IS DOWN
4. His brothers thought of killing him. THAT IS DOWN
5. He was sold into Egyptian Slavery. THAT IS DOWN.
6. He became the head at Potiphar's household. THAT IS UP.

7. Mrs Potiphar falsely accused him of rape. THAT IS DOWN

8. He was thrown into Prison for a crime he did not commit. THAT IS DOWN.

9. He interpreted dreams for powerful men in Jail. THAT IS UP

10. Despite agreement, he was forgotten when the Butler got out (for over 2years). THAT IS DOWN

11. Joseph was later remembered by the Butler and invited to the palace. THAT IS UP

12. He successfully interpreted Pharaoh's dream. THAT IS UP

13. He became the Prime Minister of Egypt. THAT IS UP

14. He delivered his family from famine. THAT IS UP

15. He died a very wealthy man. THAT IS UP

From this rough analysis of Joseph's journey from birth, to advancement and then to the pinnacle of Egypt; we can say that he advanced in the end given his starting point. But of the fifteen steps stated above, six were DOWNs and nine were Ups. This demonstrates that when Joseph was down by being sold into slavery (a natural backward move), he was actually advancing (in the spirit). Same with when he was falsely accused and then jailed for a crime he did not commit. That looked bad and negative in the natural; but still Joseph was advancing in the things of the spirit.

So when your physical state does not look like progress, don't be hard on yourself, you are advancing in the spirit…where it really matters. The physical will yield to the spiritual; it is a matter of time. Advancement is the physical progress that is evident after you have first developed spiritual Stature to overcome the opposition of the enemy. As a child of God, Satan does not want you to make progress; so he will raise stiff opposition against you. This is why you need to develop spiritual stature to win the battle in the spirit realm. Then the physical will have to give way.

Adversity is your advancement coach. When you are going through hell physically, you are still advancing. When you are afflicted, you are still advancing. When you are oppressed, you are still advancing. When your world looks like nothing good is ever going to happen, still advancing. Like Jesus, when you have been betrayed (by Judas); you are still advancing and fulfilling destiny. All these things build you up spiritually, thus helping you build the vital muscles to compel physical advancement to take place. This is the paradox of destiny; in that when you are weak, then are you strong.

So God has been developing your spiritual muscles for the season you are about to enter in your life. I am excited for you. This is your time to move to the next level. Advancement never ceases. You move from one level to another and then another. And for every level there is a new devil. You have to keep developing yourself and growing in God. You never get to a point where you stop. Physical death is the only stop to the need to keep growing in stature. As long as you are alive, you have to keep growing in stature to experience advancement to each new level in God.

Even though your physical status may appear to be declining, you are still advancing; as long as you are growing in stature. You know how a footballer retreats first (move backwards); in order to generate the momentum that will be needed to give force to the ball when he runs forward. So your apparent backward movement was part of the divine game plan. It is called "retreat to advance". It is not over for you by a long shot. You have success locked up on the inside. The world will soon hear from you, if you don't give up.

Remember the story of Gideon? He was in hiding, minding his own business. Then God showed up and called him a "Mighty man of Valour". Clearly there was a difference between Gideon's stature and status. God saw someone more that Gideon saw of himself. You are not who the world say you are. You are who God says you are. Grow where it matters. As you grow in stature; the physical will ultimately yield and your profiting will appear unto all. So on the mountain and in the valley, you are still advancing as all things are meant to work together for your good.

I hope you can now see that advancement is firstly a spiritual experience; before it becomes a physical reality.

ADVANCEMENT: SELF ANALYSIS.

Before you can begin advancing in God; you need to ask yourself why you have been stuck where you are for so long. To do this, you have to ask yourself some vital questions. You need to examine your life's performance so far. Critical examination of yourself is vital to any Advancement in God. How are you living your life? What legacy are you going to leave behind in life given the way you are going? You need to examine your Habits; Friends & Relationships; your Spending.

Philippians 3:12-17 (New Living Translation)

*¹² I don't mean to say that I have already achieved these things or that I have already reached perfection. **But I press on** to possess that perfection for which Christ Jesus first possessed me. ¹³ No, dear brothers and sisters, I have not* *achieved it, but I focus on this one thing: Forgetting the past and looking forward to what lies ahead,* 14 *I press on to reach the end of the race and receive the heavenly prize for which God, through Christ Jesus, is calling us.*

15 *Let all who are spiritually mature agree on these things. If you disagree on some point, I believe God will make it plain to you.* 16 *But we must hold on to the progress we have already made.* 17 *Dear brothers and sisters, pattern your lives after mine, and learn from those who follow our example.*

7 CRITICAL QUESTIONS YOU NEED TO ASK YOURSELF BEFORE YOU CAN EXPERIENCE ADVANCEMENT.

1. AM I LIVING, AS I OUGHT TO LIVE? Are you living as a Christian or as a Church goer?

> ***Galatians 2:20 (New King James Version)***
> 20 *I have been crucified with Christ; it is **no longer I who live**, but Christ lives in me; and the life which I now live in the flesh I **live by faith in the Son of God**, who loved me and gave Himself for me.*

The WORD Tells us how to live.
Ecclesiastes 9:9 (New King James Version)

⁹ **Live joyfully** *with the wife whom you love all the days of your vain life which He has given you under the sun, all your days of vanity; for that is your portion in life, and in the labour which you perform under the sun.*

ARE YOU LIVING JOYFULLY?
Proverbs 8:17 (New King James Version)
¹⁷ *I love those who love me, and those who* **seek me** *diligently will find me.*

ARE YOU SEEKING GOD
Are you living right? Do you embrace righteousness? If you will experience Advancement; are you living as you ought to live?

2. TO WHAT EXTENT IS MY LIFE A JUSTIFICATION FOR WHAT CHRIST DID AND THE PRICE THAT HE PAID FOR ME?
To what extent is your life a slave to sin?

To what extent are you suffering for what Christ has already paid the price for? To what extent are you constantly sick; when by His stripes you have been healed? Is the Grace of God in Vain in your life? Christ has redeemed us; but are you living in that reality?

3. TO WHAT EXTENT IS MY LIFE A TRUE REFLECTION OF MY POTENTIAL?

To what extent are you nurturing your potential?

- **Gideon (a Mighty man of valour) was in hiding.** He had to come out for his potential to be manifest.
- **David was insignificant in his father's house.** But God had to move him out for his potential to be realised.

Are what I am doing reflections of my potential in God? You need to wake up the Giant within.

4. TO WHAT EXTENT IS MY LIFE PLEASING TO GOD?

A. GOD WAS PLEASED WITH JESUS.
Matthew 3:17 (New King James Version)
17 *And suddenly a voice came from heaven, saying, "This is My beloved Son, in whom I am well pleased."*

B. JESUS DID WHAT WAS PLEASING TO GOD.

John 8:29 (New King James Version)
29 *And He who sent Me is with Me. The Father has not left Me alone, for I always do those things that please Him."*

C. ENOCH PLEASED GOD.
Hebrews 11:5 (New King James Version)
5 *By faith Enoch was taken away so that he did not see death, "and was not found, because God had taken him";[a] for before he was taken he had this testimony, that he pleased God.*

D. WHEN GOD IS PLEASE WITH YOU, HE RECOMMENDS YOU.
Matthew 17:5 (New King James Version)
5 *While he was still speaking, behold, a bright cloud overshadowed them; and suddenly a voice came out of the cloud, saying, "This is My beloved Son, in whom I am well pleased. **Hear Him!**"*

Is your life pleasing to God? To experience advancement it has to be a Yes.

5. TO WHAT EXTENT AM I A CHALLENGE, INSPIRATION AND EFFECTIVE ADVERT FOR

THE GOSPEL? *To what extent are you influencing others for God?*

Are you a good advert for the gospel? If you are accused of being a Christian will you be found guilty or innocent? You are the Christ people will see. *"Preach the gospel always and if necessary; use words".*

By their fruit we shall know them.....what fruit do you have?

6. TO WHAT EXTENT AM I A BLESSING RATHER THAN BE A BURDEN?

What contribution am I making in:

My church

My House

My Relationships

My Work or Office

If your life is not adding value to others; you will not be able to experience advancement in the Kingdom.

7. TO WHAT EXTENT IS MY LIFE PLANNED? *Is your life directed and regulated by God?*

Do you have Goals?

How disciplined are you?

EIGHT PRINCIPLES OF GOAL SETTING

1. **There are different types of Goals.**

    a. Major/Life Goals (Long-term goals)

    b. Intermediate/Staging Goals

    c. Minor Goals (Short-term goals). These are daily, weekly & monthly goals.

2. **You need to set goals for all areas of your life.**

    a. Marital Goals

    b. Ministry goals

    c. Financial goals

    d. Spiritual goals

    e. Career/business goals.

    You need to obtain necessary information that will aid your goal formation.

3. **You MUST set goals only after waiting on God and obtain clarity and direction**. Do not set goals haphazardly.

    a. Set goals only in cooperation with God.

4. **Real Goals must be specific and definite.**

    a. Ambiguous goals will fail.

    b. Tangibility is required for successful goal setting.

5. **Goals must be truthful, doable and achievable.**

    a. Don't set wild goals.

6. **Goals must be measurable and not abstract.**

    a. I will pray for 1hr or I will save 30% are measurable.

7. **Goals must be Flexible. You must give God room to manoeuvre.**

    a. Don't bind yourself to things that become a stronghold in your life.

8. **Never set goals that will take you away from God.**

CRITICAL TESTS TO ADVANCEMENT

Tests you have to pass before you can
advance in God's kingdom.

To begin your journey of advancement; you have to pass certain tests. Failing these tests will make you both unprepared for your next destination; and also make you a danger to yourself when you get there.

Genesis 1:28 : "Be fruitful" means **be productive**, "*multiply*" means **be progressive.**

There is built within everyone an innate desire to be productive and progressive. When either of them is hindered, frustration sets in. **We are designed for progress; we are wired up for movement - physically, mentally, spiritually and socially.** Something in us wants to go forward and move upward. Inside every one of us is a desire for promotion and advancement.

ULTIMATELY ALL PROMOTION & ADVANCEMENT COMES FROM GOD.

John 3:27 (New King James Version)
27 John answered and said, "A man can receive nothing unless it has been given to him from heaven.

Psalm 75:4-8 (King James Version)
4I said unto the fools, Deal not foolishly: and to the wicked, Lift not up the horn: 5Lift not up your horn on high: speak not with a stiff neck. 6For promotion cometh neither from the east, nor from the west, nor from the south. 7But God is the judge: he putteth down one, and setteth up another. 8For in the hand of the LORD there is a cup, and the wine is red; it is full of mixture; and he poureth out of the same: but the dregs thereof, all the wicked of the earth shall wring them out, and drink them.

Advancement does not come just because you want it or because you need it but it comes because you have fulfilled the criteria for advancement. In proper traditional school, you don't advance to the next grade until you have passed the test at this grade.

NO ADVANCEMENT COMES WITHOUT A TEST. The prerequisite for Advancement is that you pass some tests.

In the same token, God will require you to prove yourself at one level before you are spiritually released to go to the next. GOD DOES NOT ADVANCE YOU BECAUSE YOU NEED IT, HE PROMOTES & ADVANCES YOU BECAUSE YOU QUALIFY. So, your prime goal is to position yourself for advancement & promotion. Spiritually first before naturally.

If you are lifted up to the next level without passing the test at this level, you become dangerous - *dangerous to yourself and dangerous to others.*

WHAT WOULD YOU DO IF YOU DISCOVERED THAT THE PLANE YOU ARE ON IS GOING TO BE FLOWN BY A STUDENT PILOT WHO DROPPED OUT OF SCHOOL? How about if you were about to be operated upon by a student who did not graduate from medical school?

We only entrust our lives to people who have passed the test, proved themselves and qualify to take our lives in their hands. By the same token, every time

God advances you people's lives are in your hands. And God must ensure that you are "USER FRIENDLY" before He unleashes you on an unsuspecting world.

SEVEN TRUTHS ABOUT TESTS

1. **Tests are not pleasant**
   - o If students had a choice they would avoid the test part of the academic programme. But then, so would the teacher. Tests are stressful, strenuous and tough for everybody.
   - o God is not a sadist - He does not enjoy seeing us go through difficult times.
   - o Isaiah 63: 7 - 9 "...*In all their afflictions, He was afflicted...*"
   - o Judges 10:16 "...*His soul was grieved for the misery of Israel...*"

2. **Life tests are not pre-announced**
   Contrary to tests in the academic or corporate world, nobody sends you a letter to tell you that you are about to be tested. In fact, a lot of people go through tests without knowing that they have just been through a test.

3. **A test is not designed to teach you anything**

   You don't learn anything from a test - the lesson has been taught before. The test is designed for you to demonstrate what you have learnt. *Deuteronomy 8:2*. A test reveals what is already in you.

4. **A test is not the same as a temptation**

   A test is designed to encourage you to demonstrate your strengths. A temptation is designed to entice you to demonstrate your weakness. Notice that both of them only bring out what is already in you.

   Tests are from God and temptations are from the devil. James 1:13-17 The teacher is hoping you would pass. The tempter wants you to fail - he is looking for that faint possibility that you would slip up just so he can prove you are not that big a deal. If you claim to be strong, the devil will set out to prove that you are weak. If you say you are a patient person, the devil will look for that shred of evidence to prove that you are impatient.

5. **A temptation can also be a test**

The very same incident that the devil sets up to tempt you, God can use it to test you. God does not create hardship for you, but there are those times that He will not shield you from it. And that can be good for you, because you can kill two birds with one stone. Overcome the temptation and pass the test at the same time.

6. **When you fail a test, you usually will have to repeat it**

   You will not get promoted until you pass the test. This is why some incidents keep repeating themselves in our lives.

God is not in a hurry - He is the ancient of days, He is the eternal God - He is not growing older and time is not running out on Him. You on the other hand, don't have much time.

In school, if you get promoted when you did not pass the test at the previous grade, you will be terribly confused - you will drag the entire class back. The higher up you go in life, the less the room for mistakes - just like a triangle. There are some mistakes you can afford to make when you are 20. If you make those mistakes at 40, they will cost you.

The higher up you go, the longer the way down, and the more disastrous the fall. Now, if you do not move to the next level when you should or within reasonable time, you start to become irrelevant.

7. **No matter how hard a test is, it will be over**
So the big deal is not that the test came or it went - but what you became as a result. In Matthew 7:24-27 - the storm came and the storm went. That was not the big deal, the real issue was that one house was standing and the other was not.

James 1:2-4 : "*Consider it a sheer gift, friends when tests and challenges come at you from all sides. You know that, under pressure, your faith - life is forced into the open and shows its true colours. So don't try to get out of anything prematurely. Let it do its work so you become a better person*". [Message Bible]

Tests are supposed to make you a better person, they are supposed to become your stepping stone to promotion and advancement.

NO 1 TEST: YOU MUST PASS THE TEST OF FAITHFULNESS.

Psalm 75:6,7 - [6]*For promotion cometh neither from the east, nor from the west, nor from the south.* [7]*But God is the judge: he putteth down one, and setteth up another.*

Luke 16:10-12. - [10]*He that is faithful in that which is least is faithful also in much: and he that is unjust in the least is unjust also in much.* [11]*If therefore ye have not been faithful in the unrighteous mammon, who will commit to your trust the true riches?* [12]*And if ye have not been faithful in that which is another man's, who shall give you that which is your own?*

We live in an age where people are celebrated for their talents, abilities and achievements - but there is one quality that God values above all these - it is called FAITHFULNESS. Faithfulness has become a rarely quality amongst people.

Psalm 12:1. "*Help, Lord for the godly man ceases; for the faithful disappear from among the sons of man*".

Proverb 20:6. "*Most men will proclaim each his own goodness, but who can find a faithful man?*"

The world celebrates talent and ability. God celebrates faithfulness.

2 Timothy 2:2 - [2]*And the things that thou hast heard of me among many witnesses, the same <u>commit thou to faithful men</u>, who shall be able to teach others also.*

I Timothy 1:12 - [12]*And I thank Christ Jesus our Lord, who hath enabled me, for <u>that he counted me faithful</u>, putting me into the ministry;*

IF GOD FINDS YOU FAITHFUL, HE WILL SUPPLY THE ABILITY NEEDED FOR ADVANCEMENT.

Why does God demand that we pass the test of faithfulness before He promotes us? **Because Advancement means that more will be committed to our trust.** You are a steward of everything that you own - your job, family, ministry, money - everything! And **faithfulness is the first and highest obligation of a steward.**

1 Corinthians 4:2 "*Moreover it is required in stewards that one be found faithful*"

Proverbs 25:13 - "*...a faithful messenger refreshes the soul of his masters...*"

To be faithful means to be consistently reliable in the transaction of business, the execution of commands or the discharge of official duties. It also means to do what you are told with what has been entrusted to you.

In *Luke 16:10-12* we see the three levels of faith.

THREE LEVELS OF FAITHFULNESS

1. **Faithfulness in Small Things - vs 10**

"What is least" means that which is smallest in size, in amount, in importance, in rank and in the estimation of men.

GOD DETERMINES HOW YOU WILL PERFORM WHEN YOU ARE PROMOTED BY WATCHING HOW YOU HANDLE YOUR CURRENT POSITION.

- **How do you know if a child will take care of his first car? Simply watch what he is doing with his bicycle right now.**

- How will your staff handle the big clients? Watch them with your small clients.

- How do you know how a person will behave when they buy their own home? Watch what they are doing in the rented apartment.

"A small thing is a small thing, but faithfulness in a small thing is a big thing" - Hudson Taylor

Some people are waiting to get into the limelight before they really "perform" If you don't perform now, you won't perform then.

Zechariah 4:10 *"Who has despised the day of small things?"*

Ecclesiastes 9:10 *"Whatever your hand finds to do, do it with your might"* - put your everything into it.

The day of small things is the training ground for the day of great things, but it is also the proving ground. No matter how small what you have today, don't despise it. Be as diligent as you would if the whole world were watching - because God is watching; and He's got the whole world in His hand.

In 2 Samuel 23:1, David was described as…

- The man who was raised up on high.
- The anointed of the God of Jacob.
- The sweet psalmist of Israel.

But there was a time that the only audience he had was a flock of sheep. When he finished singing and playing on his harp, the only applause he got was the bleating of sheep. But he was faithful with those sheep - he protected them at the very risk of his own life. Little did he know that God was testing him. The greatest tests are the ones you have to pass when no one is looking.

"Prepare yourself and your day will come" - *Abraham Lincoln*

1. **Faithfulness in Finances - vs 11**

Most of us know how to be faithful with 10%, but God is not concerned about 10% of your life. Many believers are very spiritual about the 10% but they handle the 90% like carnal people. God wants to be involved in how you spend all your money. Ask yourself a simple question "How much say does God have over your finances?" At what point will you say, "Lord you are going too far - back off"? Remember to be faithful means to do what you are told with what has been committed to you.

2. Faithfulness in what is another man's - vs 12

You want to advance into your own business, home, ministry? How are you taking care of someone else's business, how are you keeping your rented flat clean, how are you handling someone else's ministry?

How do you handle stationery and office supplies at work? Do you waste it or steal it? Do you use office stamps for personal letters? Do you make personal calls on your employer's time? Do you surf the Internet when you should be working? You are stealing on two levels - first your employer's time, second his phone bill. How do you use water or electricity when you are in a hotel? When you borrow something do you return it in good condition? Do you return it at all? God wants to promote and advance you but He's watching to see if you are faithful - *Matthew 25:21*

NO 2 TEST: YOU MUST PASS THE TEST OF *MOTIVE.*

Psalm 75:6,7 ⁶ *No one from the east or the west or from the desert can exalt a man.* ⁷ *But it is God who judges: He brings one down, he exalts another.*

- o Why do you want Advancement?

- o What is your motivation?

MOTIVE IS THE COMPELLING FORCE OR REASON BEHIND A PERSON'S ACTIONS. The big question is "WHY DO YOU DO WHAT YOU DO?" **It is possible to do the right thing for the wrong reasons.** *It is possible to want to be promoted for the wrong reasons.*

Ask yourself these questions truthfully?

- Why do you serve God?
- Why do you go to church?
- Why do you pray - in private or public?
- Why are you involved in ministry - full time or not?
- Why do you give in church?
- Why do you want to marry the person you want to?
- Pastor, why do you want the anointing? - *Acts 8:18-23*
- Why do you want a big church?

In God's dealing with us, he is mostly interested in our hearts. God is not impressed with the things about us that impress other people. He knows how to sort through the façade and go to the core of the matter. Because God knows that the real you is your heart, that is the aspect of your life He relates to. God is not fooled by outward appearances. *I Samuel 16:6,7.*

Jeremiah 17:10 - *"I, the Lord search the heart and test the inner self"* - Berkeley Translation

"Who but I, the Lord, can see into man's heart and read his inner most thoughts" - **Knox Translation.**

"Only the Lord knows! He searches all hearts and examines deepest motives " - **The Living Bible.**

Before God promotes you, He applies the test of motive. **When God applies the motive test, He is not trying to <u>discover</u> what is in your heart** - *He already knows! He is only trying to <u>reveal</u> it to you so you can deal with it.*

Prosperity can reveal your true nature just as much as adversity can. *A man's greed can be demonstrated by wealth just as much as it can be demonstrated by poverty.*

TWO IMPORTANT THINGS ABOUT MOTIVES

1. You can test your own motives.

You don't need to wait for God to apply the motive test - you can examine yourself.

2 Corinthians 13:5 - ⁵ Examine yourselves as to whether you are in the faith. Test yourselves. Do you not know yourselves, that Jesus Christ is in you? – unless indeed you are disqualified.

There are two things in your life that readily reveal your motives.

   i.   Your words - *Matthew 12:34*

   ii.   Your money - *Matthew 6:21*

2. You can change your motives

If you find that your motives are not right, you can change them. Nobody is stuck with the wrong motives. "It's just the way I am" - that's a lie!

Psalm 139:23-24 - ²³Search me, O God, and know my heart: try me, and know my thoughts: ²⁴And see if there be any wicked way in me, and lead me in the way everlasting.

You can change your motives by changing the content of your heart.

Proverb 4:20-23 - *²⁰My son, attend to my words; incline thine ear unto my sayings. ²¹Let them not depart from thine eyes; keep them in the midst of thine heart. ²²For they are life unto those that find them, and health to all their flesh. ²³Keep thy heart with all diligence; for out of it are the issues of life.*

NO 3 TEST: YOU MUST PASS THE TEST OF *TIME*

In order to reveal our true motives, God supplies the test of time. In ***Ecclesiastes 3:1-8,11a,*** we see that God in His infinite wisdom has ordained a due season and an appointed time for everything.

Time is a tool in God's hands for the accomplishment of His purposes in our lives. People say, "time heals", in reality it is God who heals. He simply uses time to fulfil that purpose.

God desires to promote us and lift us up, but He uses time as a tool to bring it to pass. When a student passes an examination and is promoted to the next level, he is expected to spend some time at that level before taking the next test. **Many times we have aborted God's purpose in our lives because of our lack of patience.** At other times we have delivered His promises prematurely, and have then had to sustain them ourselves.

1. IT TAKES TIME FOR OUR BLESSINGS TO UNFOLD.

In life, some things just have to run their course and take their time. When a child is born, that baby is full of potential. But the baby needs time to grow and actualise his/her potential. Some things cannot be forced to happen quickly.

When a woman is pregnant, she has to wait nine months for her baby to be born, no matter how eager she is to have the baby. If she tries to force the baby to come earlier, she will end up with a miscarriage or a premature baby.

Faith must be coupled with patience. *Habakkuk 6:9 -15.*

2. IT TAKES TIME TO PREPARE US FOR OUR BLESSINGS

God has prepared certain things for you. *1 Corinthians 2:9*. He needs to prepare you for those blessings and preparations take time. If God does not prepare you for the blessing, you will not be able to sustain and maintain it. It is usually easier to obtain than to maintain.

In God's economy, He does not measure time in hours, days or years. He measures time in terms of the accomplishment of purpose. There are two main Greek words translated as "time" in the New Testament.

i.   "CHRONOUS" refers to a space of time or the passage of time. It is from this that we get the words chronometer, chronology etc. This speaks of time as a sequence, i.e. one minute following another. This is the commonest use of the word.

ii. "KAIROS" refers to a moment in time, a fixed time, a decisive moment when things are brought to a crisis. The right time, an opportune time, the appointed time or the fullness of time. This is used mostly in relation to God.

God considers time on the basis of when His purpose has been accomplished. He is not particularly bothered about how long or how short the amount of time that passes.

3. TIME REVEALS THE TRUE NATURE OF OUR HEARTS

Time reveals the true nature and quality of everything. A bar of gold and a banana will not survive the same period of time. Milk gets bitter with time, wine gets better with time. Some people are "milk" people and others are "wine" people.

Our stamina, our strength, our full potential is revealed in the test of time.

- o **Lesser quality clothes get worn out quicker.**
- o **Lesser quality paint fades quicker.**
- o **Lesser quality jewellery falls apart quicker.**
- o **Higher quality appliances last longer.**

When you go to a doctor for a heart check up, he hooks your heart up to a monitor and puts you on a treadmill. The first few minutes are usually okay for everyone but with time a person with a weaker heart begins to show signs of strain.

The only way to determine how strong your heart, your character is; is to put it under pressure and watch how it performs. Does it seem like God's promises are delayed in your life? You may be taking the test of time. Don't give up, your reward is on the way.

Galatians 6:9 - ⁹*And let us not be weary in well doing: for in due season we shall reap, if we faint not.*

NO 4 TEST: YOU MUST PASS THE TEST OF *SERVANTHOOD.*

*Matthew 20:20-28.*The disciples of Jesus were constantly in the habit of jockeying for position. In fact, their favourite argument was always about who would be the greatest.

An example is found in *Mark 9:33-35*.

One day, James and John, the sons of Zebedee, decided to take this matter one step further. They decided to pull a fast one on the other ten. To make it really effective, they employed the services of their mother –

Matthew 20:21-24

She came and asked for promotion for her sons. Jesus replied "You can't get promoted just like that - there is a test you must pass". James and John thought this was a test of prowess or skill or talent, so they answered, "no problem, we are ready". Vs 23 - Jesus now made them understand that this was a test of the heart; only the Father who knows the heart of all men would administer it. This really upset the rest of the disciples, they were ready to have James and John for lunch.

Jesus now calls all of them and gives them one of the greatest lessons of their entire discipleship programme.

"WHOEVER DESIRES TO BECOME GREAT AMONG YOU LET HIM BE YOUR SERVANT" vs. 26.

As a believer, you are a servant. A servant of God, yes; but still a servant! You will be a servant for the rest of your life. When you die, guess what? You will be called a servant for all eternity!

The greeting in heaven will be: *"Well done, good and faithful servant!"* **Matthew 25:21**

NO 5 TEST: YOU MUST PASS THE TEST OF CREDIBILITY.

Matthew 12:33. [33]Either make the tree good, and his fruit good; or else make the tree corrupt, and his fruit corrupt: for the tree is known by his fruit.

A tree is known by its fruit. A man is known by his works or by his credibility. Your credibility at one level of life is what opens the door to the next level. Every promotion in life is the result of passing some form of credibility test.

What does it mean to be Credible?
-Credible means to be capable of being believed. It means to be trustworthy or reliable. It derives its root from the Latin word "CREDERE" which means 'to believe'

Other people cannot earn your credibility for you. Everybody must prove himself or herself in life. *Matthew 5:16*

YOUR CREDIBILITY IS A COMBINATION OF THREE ELEMENTS

- o   What you can do – **Your Competence**

- o   How others see you – **You Reputation**

- o   Who you really are – **Your Character**

Job 8:7 - *"Though your beginning is small, yet your latter end would increase abundantly"*

Psalm 71:21 - *"You shall increase my greatness, and comfort me on every side"*

SEVEN AREAS OF YOUR LIFE THAT GOD WANTS YOU TO EXPERIENCE ADVANCEMENT.

These are the signs that you are advancing in God. As you experience the multiplication in these areas; you know your grace for advancement is in operation.

1. HE WANTS TO MULTIPLY YOUR EFFECTIVENESS.

The days of great effort and little results are over..

Five of you shall chase a hundred, and a hundred of you shall put ten thousand to flight; your enemies shall fall by the sword before you. Leviticus 26:8

2. HE WANTS TO MULTIPLY YOUR STRENGTH.

No longer will you have to face tasks and challenges for which you have no strength.

He gives power to the weak, And to those who have no might He increases strength. Isaiah 40:29

3. HE WANTS TO MULTIPLY YOUR INFLUENCE

[10] And Jabez called on the God of Israel saying, "Oh, that You would bless me indeed, and enlarge my territory, that Your hand would be with me, and that You would keep me from evil, that I may not cause pain!" So God granted him what he requested. **1 Chronicles 4:10**

[20]I have found David my servant; with my holy oil have I anointed him: [21]With whom my hand shall be established: mine arm also shall strengthen him. [22]The enemy shall not exact upon him; nor the son of wickedness afflict him. [23]And I will beat down his foes before his face, and plague them that hate him. [24]But my faithfulness and my mercy shall be with him: and in my name shall his horn be exalted. [25]I will set his hand also in the sea, and his right hand in the rivers. [26]He shall cry unto me, Thou art my father, my God, and the rock of my salvation. [27]Also I will make him my firstborn, higher than the kings of the earth. [28]My mercy will I keep for him for evermore, and my covenant shall stand fast with him. [29]His seed also will I make to endure for ever, and his throne as the days of heaven. **Psalm 89: 20-29**

4. HE WANTS TO MULTIPLY YOUR WEALTH

[1] *"Every commandment which I command you today you must be careful to observe, that you may live and multiply, and go in and possess the land of which the LORD swore to your fathers.*

"Beware that you do not forget the LORD your God by not keeping His commandments, His judgments, and His statutes which I command you today, [12] *lest – when you have eaten and are full, and have built beautiful houses and dwell in them;* [13] *and when your herds and your flocks multiply, and your silver and your gold are multiplied, and all that you have is multiplied;* Deuteronomy 8:1, 11-13

5. HE WANTS TO MULTIPLY YOUR SEED

Now may[a] He who supplies seed to the sower, and bread for food, supply and multiply the seed you have sown and increase the fruits of your righteousness, [11] *while you are enriched in everything for all liberality, which causes thanksgiving through us to God.* 2 Corinthians 9: 10,11

6. HE WANTS TO MULTIPLY HIS WONDERS IN YOUR LIFE

This will include divine health and total life provision.

³ And I will harden Pharaoh's heart, and multiply My signs and My wonders in the land of Egypt. Exodus 7:3; 11:9;

⁹ But the LORD said to Moses, "Pharaoh will not heed you, so that My wonders may be multiplied in the land of Egypt." Exodus 11:9

7. HE WANTS TO MULTIPLY YOUR DAYS

¹⁸ "Therefore you shall lay up these words of mine in your heart and in your soul, and bind them as a sign on your hand, and they shall be as frontlets between your eyes. ¹⁹ You shall teach them to your children, speaking of them when you sit in your house, when you walk by the way, when you lie down, and when you rise up. ²⁰ And you shall write them on the doorposts of your house and on your gates, ²¹ that your days and the days of your children may be multiplied in the land of which the LORD swore to your fathers to give them, like the days of the heavens above the earth. Deuteronomy 11:18-21

IT IS TIME TO STEP INTO THE COVENANT OF MULTIPLICATION AS YOU ADVANCE IN LIFE.

LIVING AND EXPERIENCING ADVANCEMENT

Critical questions that signposts advancement

1 Peter 5:10
¹⁰ *But may the God of all grace, who called us to His eternal glory by Christ Jesus, after you have suffered a while, perfect, establish, strengthen, and settle you.*

Job 8:7 - *"Though your beginning is small, yet your latter end would increase abundantly"*

Psalm 71:21 - *"You shall increase my greatness, and comfort me on every side"*

If you will experience advancement:
1. WHAT DO YOU NEED TO KNOW?
2. WHAT DO YOU NEED TO DO?
3. WHAT DO YOU NEED TO SAY?

4. WHERE DO YOU NEED TO GO?
5. WHO DO YOU NEED TO KNOW?

1. WHAT DO YOU NEED TO KNOW?

There are **Five** crucial things you need to know.

A. **THERE IS A <u>PARTICULAR TYPE OF PERSON</u> GOD WANT YOU TO BE.**

What effort are you making in this direction?

God wants you to be like Jesus.

"...and have put on the new man who is renewed in knowledge according to the image of Him who created him. ***Col. 3:10***

[6] He who says he abides in Him ought himself also to walk just as He walked. ***1 John 2:6***

To what extent are you making an effort to be who God wants you to be? What is the distance between who you are today and who God want you to be.

2 Corinthians 3:18 *[18] But we all, with unveiled face, beholding as in a mirror the glory of the Lord, are being* *transformed into the same image from glory to glory, just as by the Spirit of the Lord.*

The more you are like Him; the more you can do what He did.

The second thing you need to know is:
B. THERE IS <u>A PLACE</u> GOD WANTS YOU TO BE.
There is a place: **Physically; Spiritually; Economically; Materially & Emotionally**.
GOD HAS HIS OWN PLACE:

For behold, the LORD is coming out of His place; He will come down, And tread on the high places of the earth.
Micah 1:3

God wants you to be in a place of
  o   Victory; A place of always above and never beneath.
  o   Where no weapon against you will prosper.
  o   Being in Health
  o   A place of all sufficiency in all thing.
What effort are you making to get to the place God want you to BE? **You need to be hungry and thirsty for this place.**

The third thing you need to know is:

C. THERE ARE <u>CERTAIN THINGS</u> GOD WANTS YOU TO POSSESS/INHERIT IN HIM

THERE ARE THINGS GOD WANTS YOU TO HAVE AS HIS CHILDREN. You need to understand this to activate His grace for Advancement.

Luke 15:31 (New King James Version)
31 *"And he said to him, 'Son, you are always with me, and all that I have is yours.*

Psalm 84:11 (New King James Version)
11 *For the LORD God is a sun and shield; The LORD will give grace and glory; No good thing will He withhold from those who walk uprightly.*

John 10:10 (New King James Version)
10 *The thief does not come except to steal, and to kill, and to destroy. I have come that they may have life, and that they may have it more abundantly.*
There are dimensions of God many of us do not know yet. There are higher Vista of Glory.

Psalm 90:17 (King James Version) 17*And let the beauty of the LORD our God be upon us: and establish thou the work* *of our hands upon us; yea, the work of our hands establish thou it.*

The forth thing you need to know is:

D. THERE ARE <u>CERTAIN THINGS</u> GOD WANT YOU TO DO.

There are things God want you to do for HIM:
For His Kingdom, for your Brethren; for your Church; for your family, for Yourself.

God want you to:

- Live right; Serve your world;
- Preach the gospel with your lifestyle
- Be a blessing; Love your neighbour
- Be obedient & Operate in Faith

Your ability to do what He wants you to do will determine your advancement in the Kingdom.

The 5ᵗʰ thing you need to know is:

E. THERE IS <u>A PURPOSE</u> GOD WANTS YOU TO FULFIL.

What is God's Purpose for your life? Do you know your purpose on this earth? You cannot experience Advancement, if you are ignorant of your purpose.

Jeremiah 1:5 (King James Version)
⁵*Before I formed thee in the belly I knew thee; and before you came forth out of the womb I sanctified you, and I ordained you a prophet unto the nations.*

Acts 15:18 (King James Version)
¹⁸*Known unto God are all his works from the beginning of the world.*

Do you have a purpose statement for your life? What is driving your actions daily?
CHRIST HAD A PURPOSE. SO MUST YOU.

1 John 3:8 (King James Version)
⁸*He that committeth sin is of the devil; for the devil sinneth from the beginning. For <u>this purpose</u> the Son of God was manifested, that he might destroy the works of the devil.*

These are the FIVE things you need to Know; if you are to experience Advancement in God.

If you will experience advancement:
2. WHAT DO YOU NEED TO DO?
There are **Five** crucial things you need to do.
    A. YOU MUST LEARN TO WALK IN LOVE.

The enemy attacks us in the area of our love walk **because our power is in the love of God.** We must understand who God really is; He is love (1 John 4:7-18).

    a. The words *love* and *God* can be used interchangeably.

For whosoever is born of (love) overcometh the world; this is the victory that overcometh the world even our faith (1 John 5:4).

Cultivating the love of God in your life and sharing it with others is the key to experiencing the fullness of His power. Without love, the gifts of God are useless. And without those gifts in operation in your life, you are ultimately useless to God. Love is the master key to unlocking the things of God.

In the last days, the love of many will grow cold (Matthew 24:4-12, *AMP*).

Many people, including Christians, are abandoning the "love realm" in order to operate in the "sense realm." Many are convinced that walking in love is useless because of the sinful and lawless times they are living in. **Your *vertical* relationship with God will determine the effectiveness of your *horizontal* relationship with others.**

By perfecting your love walk with others, you ultimately perfect your love walk with God. When you choose not to love others, you allow fear to affect you, thereby giving Satan access to your life. Love enables you to live as a conqueror in the world.

The God-kind of love is not human. His love is supernatural and "Holy Spirit-injected." The human kind of love is conditional. God's love is unconditional. When you become born again, the Holy Spirit "injects," or pours, God's love into your heart (Romans 5:5, *AMP*). Loving others is proof that you are born again. **You cannot separate God from His love (1 John 4:16).** Love is the root to all that is God's (anointing, miracles, wealth, healing, etc.) and all that makes up God. To love God is to love His Word and align your life according to what it says.

You must love others even when it's not easy to do so. Your love walk must be based on what the Word of

God says, even when it instructs you to love others in unconventional ways.

Matthew 5:43-44: *"Ye have heard that it hath been said, Thou shalt love thy neighbour, and hate thine enemy. But I say unto you, Love your enemies, bless them that curse you, do good to them that hate you, and pray for them which despitefully use you, and persecute you."*

Ask the Holy Spirit to help you. Loving others even when it hurts positions you to live the "too much" lifestyle-a life of too much favour, anointing, wealth, goodness and health. Love will quench the spirit of strife. God's love in you will compel your enemies to constantly seek after you. They will want to be in contact with that love. Don't allow the fear of rejection to stop you from loving anyone.

Christ will return for a people who have made walking in love a lifestyle. Your goal is to increase and abound in the love of God toward *all* people. The perfection of your love walk will not happen overnight; love is cultivated over time. Jesus will manifest Himself in your life when you love Him enough to obey His Word (John 14:22-23). Keeping

God's Word requires that you don't obey Him just to get something from Him. Obey Him because you love Him.

Become *rooted* and *grounded* in the love of God. It will be the "anchor" that will enable you to survive the storms of life (Ephesians 3:17). To fully understand and walk in the love of God, pray that you receive a *revelation* of His love. Once you receive a revelation of love, you will understand how to perfect the principles of God concerning other spiritual matters. Be on your guard; Satan will attempt to hinder you in your pursuit of the God-kind of love.

THE LOVE OF GOD WILL FLUSH OUT ALL FEAR AND GIVE US THE ABILITY TO ADVANCE AND GET RESULTS IN OUR LIVES.

*The 2nd thing you **need to do** is:*
B. YOU MUST COMMIT TO EXCELLENCE.
Daniel Distinguished himself by excellence.
" It pleased Darius to set over the kingdom one hundred and twenty satraps, to be over the whole kingdom; 2 and over these, three governors, of whom Daniel was one, that the satraps might give account to them, so that the king would

suffer no loss. [3] *Then this* **_Daniel distinguished himself above the governors and satraps,_** *because an excellent spirit was in him; and the king gave thought to setting him over the whole realm".* **Dan.6:1-3**

Many believers have sadly developed Bad Reputation that makes Advancement difficult; especially in the Marketplace.

The Spirit of Excellence

Ps. 8:1 - *How excellent is thy name.*

His very name is excellent, and the very nature of God is hidden in the names of God, and His very nature is Excellence. Looking through the Word of God, everything that He created was Excellent. He made us excellent, and we are conforming to His image.

There is an example in the Bible of a man of excellence. His name was Daniel.

Daniel 5:12
Because an excellent spirit, knowledge, and understanding to interpret dreams, clarify riddles, and solve knotty problems were found in this same Daniel...

What was found in Daniel? An excellent spirit – *the Spirit of Excellence…* One of the results of having the Spirit of Excellence can be found in Daniel 1:20

Daniel 1:17-20

17 As for these four youths, God gave them knowledge and skill in all learning and wisdom, and Daniel had understanding in all [kinds of] visions and dreams. 18 Now at the end of the time which the king had set for bringing [all the young men in], the chief of the eunuchs brought them before Nebuchadnezzar. 19 And the king conversed with them, and among them all none was found like Daniel, Hananiah, Mishael, and Azariah; therefore they were assigned to stand before the king. 20 And in all matters of wisdom and understanding concerning which the king asked them, he found them ten times better than all the [learned] magicians and enchanters who were in his whole realm.

When you have the Spirit of Excellence, it is not hidden. The world can see it. It is seen by the world. Look at Daniel 1:20 – In ALL matters, they were found 10 times better. Now, what made these men 10 times better than all the other learned scholars and magicians? They were flowing in the Spirit of Excellence. When you catch the Spirit of Excellence, you stand out from the crowd! The world says "if they want me to do more, they better pay me more, and until they pay me more, I'm not doing any more...". The Spirit of Excellence says to do more now. And when you do more now, you will end up making more.

So what is the Spirit of Excellence?

Excellence is the image of God: **God is NOT mediocre.**

Mediocre = of moderate or low quality, value, ability, or performance

God is the very top, the very definition of excellence. Any area of our lives, anything that we do, if it is done mediocre, we are not conforming to the image of Christ. Whether it is our job, an area that we volunteer to help the church, any area. If this is mediocre, we are not conforming to the Spirit of Excellence. If you make a commitment to be somewhere or do something, and you don't do it, you are not conforming to the Spirit of Excellence. We should do things as "unto the Lord". As we do things "unto the Lord", we should do those things with excellence. Defining "unto the Lord" could be "Spirit of Excellence".

If you had an appointment with the Lord, would you show up? Would you be on time? How would you dress? If you were going to be late, and it was unavoidable, would you call Him? We can't say that we are doing something "unto the Lord", unless we are really doing it "unto the Lord". If Jesus was sitting here, would we still be doing it the same way? God is not mediocre, He is not half way.

Excellence is a Spirit *(a characteristic, or an attitude, not another spirit like the Holy Spirit)*

Excellence is not taught, it is caught. You have to want to catch the Spirit of Excellence. You have to predetermine in your heart that you want to catch it, or you won't. The Spirit of Excellence can be applied to your work, to your ministry, to anything that you put your hand to do. If we are not doing it with the Spirit of Excellence – God is not in it. God is in what you do in the same measure as the excellence you do it with… If you want more of His glory in your life, this is one way to see His glory. Do it with excellence. God doesn't do anything, unless it is with excellence. Nothing in creation was created without excellence, and He doesn't associate with anything below excellence.

Excellence always stands out in a crowd, because people are not accustomed to seeing it. It is a rarity in today's world. Excellence is a destination and a direction, not a state of being. It is where we are heading. Nobody, short of God, has arrived at excellence. We are to continually strive for more excellence in what we do. Excellence does not work from the outside-in, but from the inside-out. It starts at the core, at the heart, and works out. Excellence is a battle between your flesh and your spirit. Your flesh will keep you in mediocrity every time, but your Spirit was created by the Lord, and is already an excellent Spirit. The problem is that it does not have dominance. If you are mediocre in what you do, your flesh is ruling – not your Spirit-man.

Excellence makes us judge ourselves. We have to judge ourselves to determine if we are operating in Excellence. The flesh will tell you "I want to judge others and not me..." The spirit will tell you "I'm allowed to judge me, and I won't be distracted about anybody else...". Excellence is a habit. We have to strive for excellence. It is not the achieving of excellence that becomes a habit, but the continual act of striving for it. Until we habitually strive for excellence, we will not be able to catch the Spirit of Excellence.

Excellence is a reputation, and so is mediocrity.

For us to begin to flow and operate in excellence, we must begin by judging ourselves. We must examine ourselves and determine the areas that we can and should improve upon. We don't want to go our entire lives living a mediocre life, when we could have had the fullness of God and His glory by operating in excellence. We must compare the way we are doing what we are doing to the way that it could be done. If we are greeting, or ushering, we should compare how we perform the service with how it CAN be done. We must compare our present standard with the potential that God has uniquely and lovingly placed within each one of us.

Striving for excellence helps us fulfil the potential that God already has on the inside. God already has a plan for us, but most of the time, we don't fulfil the plan because we never reach the true potential that we have inside.

*The 3rd thing you **need to do** is:*

C. YOU MUST COMMIT TO SPIRITUAL WARFARE.

As you physically advance in life, you increasingly enter terrains that only fewer people have been before. **So for every level there is a new devil.** You need to win the battle in the spirit to advance in the physical. You need to be strengthened with might by His spirit in your inner man.

For we wrestle not against flesh and blood, but against principalities, against powers, against the rulers of the darkness of this world, against spiritual wickedness in high places, Eph 6:12.

This is a personal commitment. **Wrestling is not a team sport.** You understand that in team sports, you have help as Joab said to his brother Abishai in 1CHRO 19:12, *"And he said, If the Syrians be too strong for me, then thou shalt help me; but if the children of Ammon be too strong for thee, then I will help thee."* That is a team war.

In a ball game, you see teams. If one seems to be overcome, there is another member of the team who can relieve him from combat. Then they are able to recover strength and go again.

In a wrestling match it is one-to-one. When we start dealing with this subject of wrestling with Satan, we are dealing one-on-one. There are no teams.

In 1 Samuel 17:8, we read about Goliath and David. LET US Stop and ANALYSE the armies of Israel. They were confronted by the armies of the Philistines. When they were confronted, Goliath went out and asked, "Why put these armies in array? This would put our whole armies in jeopardy. Let me have one man, and I'll war with one man. If I win, you'll be servants.

If your man wins, we'll be servants." Goliath suggested this in **1 Samuel 17:8,** "*And he stood and cried unto the armies of Israel, and said unto them, Why are ye come out to set your battle in array? Am not I a Philistine, and ye servants to Saul? Choose you a man for you, and let him come down to me.*" He was saying to put the battle in array one man to one man.

That would be a very personal warfare. We have to understand that Goliath is a type of **"the old man of sin."** Warfare is going to become a very personal matter between you and **"the old man of sin."**

You will find that you are fighting a personal warfare, one-to-one. We don't go in as an army or a unit. We don't go in to try and gain a victory as a combined, organized team. **We must go alone**. And we can only win, largely due to our personal actions. We find we are in a one to one battle. When an army engages in a battle, some men may come out without a scratch. When the battle is one-on-one, you are the sole object of your challenger's fury. Your challenger's fury is directed to you personally. You are the sole object.

In 1 Samuel 17:9 we read, *"If he be able to fight with me, and to kill me, then will we be your servants: but if I prevail against him, and kill him, then shall ye be our servants, and serve us."* Think of the challenge for David. He had to go face Goliath alone. They had the understanding that if he was slain, the armies of Israel, the armies of the Lord, would become servants to "the old man of sin."

That was a tremendous challenge. He went in the

name of the Lord. It will be in the name of the Lord that you and I will come against "the old man of sin." We must come against Goliath.

You give Satan a dangerous advantage if you see his wrath and fury against the saints in general, and not against yourself in particular. You give him a horrible advantage, because you are caught off guard. He can have some tremendous advantages on you before you stop to realize you are his target. It is you personally. **Satan hates me!** Satan accuses me! Satan tempts me! Don't look at this in general terms, but in personal terms.

When we talk about "wrestling," we have to understand that it is not a team sport. It is a one-to-one battle. It becomes so personal that Satan hates me! That temptation is for my fall. The battle against Goliath becomes a warfare of mine. I have to fight with Goliath, and then I realize the magnitude of that battle.

You're in a wrestling match and you make physical contact. That opponent actually takes hold of you; he has a hold of you with an objective to put you down and gain a victory over you. It becomes a wrestling match. You either resist or fall shamefully at his feet. If you think you can go through these wrestling matches without resisting the devil, you are going to fall shamefully at his feet. He is going to crumble you.

We have to understand what we read in James 4:7, *"Submit yourselves therefore to God. Resist the devil, and he will flee from you."*

Our text says, "WE WRESTLE." The apostle thereby included himself. **THERE ISN'T ONE PERSON WHO IS EXCLUDED FROM THIS.** The quarrel of Satan is with every saint. Satan is not afraid to quarrel with the pastor. He is not too proud to quarrel with the poorest saint. Satan doesn't forget anybody's address. This wrestling match is going to include everyone. The day you got saved, Satan got your number.

As we grow in grace, the spiritual warfare only increases. As we go forward and become mature Christians, the warfare doesn't get won; it gets greater. In Galatians 5:17 we read, *"For the flesh lusteth against the Spirit, and the Spirit against the flesh: and these are contrary the one to the other: so that ye cannot do the things that ye would."*

Draw nigh unto God, and he'll draw nigh unto thee. So to advance in the Kingdom, we have to wrestle successfully.

*The 4ᵗʰ thing you **need to do** is:*
D. YOU MUST COMMIT TO INTEGRITY AND ETHICAL STANDARDS.

*Psalm 51:6 (**New King James Version**) -* ⁶ *Behold, <u>You desire truth in the inward parts</u>, And in the hidden part You will make me to know wisdom.*

You are the Jesus/Christ many will see; so YOU HAVE TO COMMIT TO WINNING BY RIGHTEOUSNESS THROUGH OBEDIENCE.

Our obedience to the moral principles of the Bible really boils down to one word—honour. When we honour God, His Word holds weight in our lives. We cannot say we truly love Him without obeying what He tells us to do. In John 14:15 Jesus says, *"If ye love me, keep my commandments."* Obeying God is the acid test of our love for Him. On a practical level, that means if

He says we should not dishonour our bodies by engaging in sexual sin, we refrain from fornication. If He says we must renew our minds to acquire His thoughts, we make it our priority. We simply do what He says because He loves us.

In order to maintain moral integrity in today's society, it is going to be imperative that we absolutely make God's Word our final authority. We must believe with every fibre of our being that the Bible is right and that God doesn't change His mind about what has been written. The moment we begin to accept contradictory ideas about what is right or wrong, we are setting ourselves up for compromise. We must remain established in the truths found in the Scriptures at all costs.

Studying and meditating on the Word are also critical to developing a consciousness of what pleases God. As we renew our minds according to Romans 12:1, 2, we will be able to prove what the perfect will of God is. Colossians 3:1-10 discuss how we are to embrace higher ways of thinking and behaving, while letting go of the immoral lifestyles we once lived. I believe this is one of the primary ways we are able to be effective witnesses for the Lord.

When the people in our circles of influence begin to see that we no longer engage in the things we used to do, because of our integrity and ethical standards, it will really have an impact. The best way to introduce others to the Lord is to let them see what He has done in us. This even speaks louder than our words. This is a crucial requirement for advancement.

*The 5th thing you **need to do** is:*
E. YOU MUST NEVER GIVE UP.
Be Persistent. Be consistent. Be determined

CHALLENGES WILL COME ; BUT MAKE YOUR MIND UP NEVER TO GIVE UP.
I recently read this story about Winston Churchill who was giving a commencement address. "After enduring a lengthy introduction, Churchill is reported to have risen from his seat, strode to the podium and stared fixedly at his audience of new graduates. "Never give up!" he pronounced solemnly. Churchill then turned, walked back to his chair and sat down. As the stunned students momentarily sat in silence, Churchill, with

perfect timing, once again rose from his chair, returned to the podium and again announced, "Never give up!"

Now, terrified they might respond improperly, the audience never uttered a squeak as their speaker once again returned to his seat. Sure enough, Churchill returned to the podium again, and again and yet again - five times - each time delivering his single-minded message, "Never give up!" At last, feeling he had exhausted his audience and driven home his point, Churchill himself did give up and returned to the podium no more. But you can be sure that every graduate in that audience never forgot that speech and never forgot that he or she was to "never give up!"'

Galatians 6:9 *"...for at the proper time we will reap a harvest if we do not give up."*

What does it mean? The scripture tells us that if we do not give up on we will surely see the reward of it. For example the farmer sows his seed and takes the little grown stuff and plants it in the properly ploughed field. He does not see the grains immediately, he waits for the rain and the shine at the proper times and then a harvest, during harvest it is not what he sowed but several measures more than what he had sown. If this is true for a farmer I am sure the same principle applies for us too. The only thing is to wait patiently until we see results.

When you have fulfilled the spiritual requirement for advancement; just wait on God for the physical manifestation will surely come.

If you will experience advancement:
3. WHAT DO YOU NEED TO SAY?
There are **THREE** crucial things you need to say.

A. YOU NEED TO SPEAK THE LANGUAGE REFLECTING YOUR NEXT LEVEL, BEFORE IT MANIFESTS.

You need speak of where you are going and not where you are coming from. David said to Goliath..."*Today I will cut of your head and feed your body to the birds of the air*". But all he had on him at that time was just a sling and five stones. SO HOW WAS HE GOING TO CUT OFF GOLIATH'S HEAD SINCE HE HAD NO SWORD? David was speaking of the destination before he arrived there.

Most of us hope and expect to significantly alter our

results in our marketplace but continue to use the same 'market language' that holds us back. And until the language changes, change in results will be almost impossible. So if you're not achieving the results that befit you, or, you find yourself climbing the wall of success only to periodically hang on for dear life, then examine just one thing: *Your Market Language.*

We'll define 'market language' as the words and conversations you engage in throughout the market place of your life, which includes customers, prospects, suppliers, managers, family and of course, self. Optimized, this language can take us to new levels of proficiency and enrichment. Unexamined, this language can be limiting - and we never know it. So you need to develop marketplace lingo relevant to your area of expertise. You do not want to go to a business meeting and keep saying "Amen" after every word. Developing the language appropriate for the marketplace prepares you to engage with it successfully and trigger advancement.

The 2nd thing you need to say is:
B. YOU NEED TO CONTUNUALLY SPEAK THE WORD OF GOD OVER ALL YOUR SITUATIONS.

The World is already full of negative confessions; so you must not join them. Do not fear their fear. Do not talk their negative talk. Use your words as instruments of transformation. Changing your confession will aid your advancement.

Three penniless knights were lost on their return home from their pilgrimage to the Holy Land. They were caught in a violent rainstorm that lasted for seven days. During the first day of their ordeal they crossed a creek bed in the inky, black of night. Suddenly they heard a voice that commanded, "Pick up some of the pebbles and you will be glad and sad." The first weary knight thought this directive was ridiculous, so he refused. The second knight reached down, picked up a hand full of the stones and put them in his pack.

The third knight dismounted and then stuffed an empty saddlebag with the stones. Six arduous days later the weather broke. Finally they were able to make camp and rest. On opening his saddlebag, the third knight discovered that it was filled with precious jewels. His joy was boundless. The second knight found a handful of precious stones in

his pack. He was glad he had them, but sad he did not have more. The first knight was
very sad because he was still penniless.

Believer's declarations and confessions is like a hidden treasure when we have lost our way in the storms of life. We will be sad, sad and glad, or overjoyed depending on our willingness to claim its riches. You cannot attract into your life what you have not confessed as so. You need to learn to speak the truth of the word, regardless of physical realities on the ground. Choose to believe the report of the Lord. Continually speak the word of God and your physical situation will be compelled to respond.

*The 3rd thing you **need to say** is:*
C. YOU NEED TO CONSTANTLY SPEAK TO GOD IN PRAYERS
God needs earthly licence for heaven's intervention. This is called PRAYER.
Who knows what God may accomplish through prayer? The prophet Elisha experienced the miraculous protection of God as the result of prayer. The king of Syria sought to kill Elisha, who kept telling the Israelite army his every move. When the Syrian

king discovered Elisha in Dothan, he sent a huge army to surround the city.

Early the next morning, Elisha saw the army ready to attack. When his frightened servant asked Elisha what they should do, Elisha asked God to open the eyes of the young man. Immediately the servant could see the hillside around Elisha filled with horses and chariots of fire—a hedge of angels.

As the Syrian army approached, Elisha prayed, "Strike this people, I pray, with blindness" (2 Kin. 6:18). Elisha then led the blind army all the way to Samaria before God opened their eyes, again through the prayers of Elisha! What miracles might God want to do through your prayers? Prayer is key to Advancement.

If you will experience advancement:
4. WHERE DO YOU NEED TO GO?
There are **THREE** crucial places you need to go.

A. YOU NEED ABIDE IN THE SECRET PLACE OF THE MOST HIGH.

You must cultivate the presence of the Holy Spirit. That is where there is protection and guidance for advancement.

Mankind was created to function in the presence of the Lord.

Psalm 91- 1 He who dwells in the secret place of the Most High Shall abide under the shadow of the Almighty.

Psalm 31:20 (NKJV- 20 You shall hide them in the secret place of Your presence, From the plots of man; You shall keep them secretly in a pavilion From the strife of tongues.

The presence of God is His secret place. You need to cultivate the presence of God and walk in that reality. It is in His presence that you get the divine keys and secrets that lead to advancement.

*The 2nd place you **need to go** is:*

B. YOU NEED TO GO TO WHERE THE VOICE OF GOD DIRECTS.

The voice of God is the greatest Assets to a believer's destiny. Which voice are you following?

DO NOT confuse Noise with Voice.

6 The sound of noise from the city! A voice from the temple! The voice of the LORD, Who fully repays His enemies!
Isaiah 66:6

It is in His presence that you obtain divine guidance. The leadings of the spirit is the greatest asset to a believer's destiny. This helps you to develop stature in the spirit that will ultimately command physical advancement.

*The 3rd place you **need to go** is:*

C. YOU NEED TO GO TO THE PLACE OF REST IN GOD.

To experience Advancement you need to learn to rest. Avoid Burnout. (Physical Rest). You need to also learn to cast all your cares on God. (Spiritual Rest). You rest in the spirit after you have seen God's completed work in heavenly places. This should make physical rest easier as you will no longer be afraid of what you can see in the natural. Seeing the finished work of God; gives rest needed to promote advancement in your life.

"Therefore, let us fear lest, while a promise remains of entering His rest, any one of you should seem to have come short of it. 2 For indeed we have had good news preached to us, just as they also; but the word they heard did not profit them, because it was not united by faith in those who heard. 3 For we who have believed enter that rest, just as He has said, "AS I SWORE IN MY WRATH, THEY SHALL NOT ENTER MY REST," although His works were finished from the foundation of the world. 4 For He has thus said somewhere concerning the seventh day, "AND GOD RESTED ON THE SEVENTH DAY FROM ALL HIS WORKS"; 5 and again in this passage, "THEY SHALL NOT ENTER MY REST." 6 Since therefore it remains for some to enter it, and those who formerly had good news preached to them failed to enter because of disobedience". Hebrews 4:1–6 (ESV)

There is a rest open to you today. God offers rest. The door is not shut. The time is not past. You have not missed your last opportunity. Ah, but someone says, "Yes, a rest remains for the people of God — but not for me." But I answer, do not rule yourself out. Look at verse 3; *"We who have believed enter that rest."* There is one door to the safe, peaceful, happy rest of God — the door of faith.

Anyone who puts faith in God's promises bought for us by the blood of Jesus, and is diligent not to throw that faith away, *is* a part of the people of God. So on behalf of God, I call you today, put your trust in the promise of God's rest and you will be shielded from the earthly pressure and tricks for advancement. You will instead develop in stature thus compelling your physical advancement to manifest.

If you will experience advancement:

5. WHO DO YOU NEED TO KNOW?
There are **FOUR** crucial people you need to know.

A. YOU NEED TO KNOW GOD INTIMATELY
Your level of advancement in life is linked with how well you know God. This is the only way to avoid the manipulations of the enemy.

When you develop an intimate relationship with God, you will become wise, and wisdom will be given to you to understand and help you overcome the trials and temptations that come your way every day.

"[For my determined purpose is] that I may know Him [that I may progressively become more deeply and intimately acquainted with Him, perceiving and recognizing and understanding the wonders of His Person more strongly and more clearly]." (Philippians 3:10 AMP)

To know God intimately should be the number one priority in every born-again believer's life. We were created to fellowship with God and nothing else will satisfy that longing for Him. We should diligently seek Him with a whole heart, then we will come to know Him in a more intimate way. We seek Him by spending time with Him in prayer and in His word. The word seek means to crave, pursue and go after with all of your might. Jesus said that we are to seek God first and then everything that we need will be given to us. When we put God first in our lives, He will supply our every need.

What a privilege it is to be able to fellowship with God any time of the day or night! We can be as close to God as we want to be. Getting to know God is like getting to know anyone. We have to take the time to develop our relationship with our heavenly Father. We have to fellowship with Him to experience intimacy with Him.

We become like the people we spend time with. We should spend time with our heavenly Father so we can become more like Him.

God will reveal His unconditional love for us as we fellowship with Him. Our heavenly Father loves and cherishes us and has good plans for our lives. He wants to have unbroken fellowship with His children. If we will spend an hour or two out of every twenty-four with Him, we will be changed and empowered by His presence.

Paul said that we should ask God to give us wisdom and revelation that we may know Him better. Knowing God is a process of growing spiritually. He will teach us His will and ways as we spend time with Him. He will grow us up into His image as we yield to Him. God dwells in us and He wants us to dwell in His presence. His desire for us is that we would abide in the place of communion with Him and total dependency upon Him. He wants to bless and prosper us in every area of our lives.

We should continually desire to fellowship with God and to know Him more and more intimately. Inner fulfilment comes only through time spent with God. We must maintain a vital union with our heavenly Father on a daily basis in order to grow spiritually and live victoriously! This is the basis for advancement.

*The 2nd person you **need to know** is:*

B. YOU NEED TO KNOW YOUR GOD-SEND MENTORS.

The Instruction you follow will determine the future you create. Mentorship is knowledge without the Pain of Discovery. You must make an investment in Mentorship

- o What Books are you reading?
- o What CDs/Tapes are you listening to?
- o Whose meetings are you attending?
- o Whose Counsel do you listen to?

Being mentored is a difficult and often frustrating process, as those who are older and wiser push us to be more than the sum of our failures and drive us to direct our lives in ways that honour Christ more and more every day. Being a mentor is also very important, and is much more challenging than being mentored. It requires a great deal of patience, a love for the person being mentored by you, and a love of Jesus that overrides everything.

The effective mentor is a real person sharing real life experiences, struggles, and wisdom. You need to know who your mentors are and submit to them in order to learn from them. You do not have enough time on earth to say you want to make all your own mistakes. You are supposed to learn from other people. There is no point re-inventing the will, if you can learn from those ahead of you. This contributes to developing spiritual stature necessary for physical advancement.

*The 3rd person you **need to know** is:*

C. YOU NEED TO KNOW YOUR COVENANT RELATIONSHIPS

The Bible says; "Walk with the wise and you will be wise, but a companion of fools shall be destroyed". The truth is that nobody succeeds alone. God has put some of what you need to fulfil your assignment in some other vessel. This way we will need each other. Nobody is an island. So to succeed you need to know those God have sent to you. You need to be aware of your covenant relationships. This is beyond mere friendships; but requires a need spiritual commitment to each other. You need to have a few people in your life that fits this description.

Our relationship with God is personal; but we need the input of faithful friends in covenant relationship to overcome some of the obstacles on the road to destination Advancement.

The 4th person you **need to know** *is:*
D. YOU NEED TO KNOW YOURSELF.
THE POWER OF IDENTITY. Who are you in Christ Jesus? What are your strengths and weaknesses? What do you need to work on in your weaknesses to make you a better person? How do you develop better relationship skills?

If you don't know who you are, you will answer to any name you are called. Knowing who you are in Christ; strengthens your faith and your resolve to face down the enemy. You cannot advance in God, if you suffer from Identity crisis.

THIS IS OUR DESTINATION:
Habakkuk 2:14 (New King James Version)

[14] *For the earth will be filled   With the knowledge of the glory of the LORD,   As the waters cover the sea.*

When we all advance then we bring the glory of the Lord to bear on our world. God bless you and I will see you at the top.

Books by Pastor Charles Omole

1. **Church, It's time to Fly** -- *Learning to fly on Eagles Wing.*

2. **How to Avoid Getting Hurt in Church** -- *13 Steps that will protect you and help create an atmosphere for breakthroughs.*

3. **Must I go to Church** -- *8 Reasons why you must attend Church.*

4. **Freedom from Condemnation** -- *Breaking free from the burden and weight of sin.*

5. **I cannot serve a big God and remain small**

6. **How to start your own business**

7. **How to Make Godly Decisions**

8. **How to avoid financial collapse**

9. **Let Brotherly love continue:** *An insight into love and companionship.*

10. **Breaking out of the debt trap**

11. **Common Causes of Unanswered Prayer.**

12. **How to Argue with God and Win** -- *Biblical strategies on getting God's attention for all your circumstances all of the time*

13. **Avoiding Power Failure**-- *How to generate spiritual power for daily success and victorious living.*

14. **How long should I continue to pray when I don't see an answer?**

15. **SUCCESS KILLERS:** *Seven Habits of Highly Ineffective Christians.*

16. **The Financial Resource Handbook** – UK Edition

17. **Divine Strategies for uncommon breakthroughs:** *Living in the Reality of the Supernatural:*

18. **Keys to Divine Success**

For more information about our ministry, world outreaches and a free catalogue of our media and study materials, please write to:

Winning Faith Outreach Ministries
151 Mackenzie Road
London. N7 8NF
UNITED KINGDOM
www.charlesomole.org
info@charlesomole.org

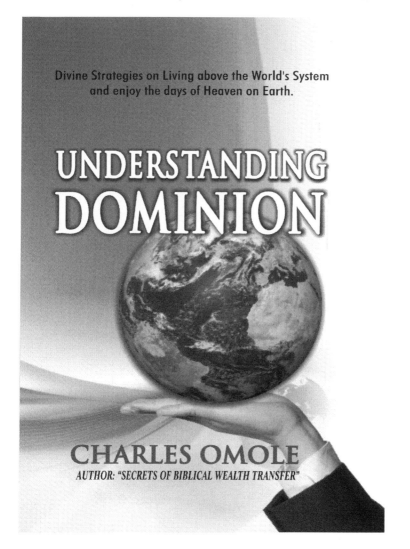

Divine Strategies on Living above the World's System and enjoy the days of Heaven on Earth.

UNDERSTANDING DOMINION

CHARLES OMOLE
AUTHOR: "SECRETS OF BIBLICAL WEALTH TRANSFER"

A Definitive Christian Guide
to Biblical Economics

PROSPERITY
Unleashed

CHARLES OMOLE

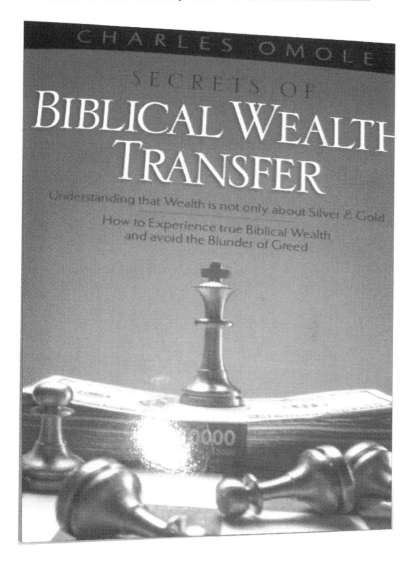

CHARLES OMOLE

AUTHOR: KEYS TO DIVINE SUCCESS

WRONG
Thoughts
WRONG
Emotions &
WRONG
Living

— Divine strategies for developing a healthy mind.
— How your thoughts dictate your realities & dominate your lifestyle.
— Possessing your destiny in God and unlocking your future
through the Power of a renewed mind.

THE KINGDOM ECONOMIC EMPOWERMENT SERIES

Your Broad Guide to Living above the World's
Economic System & Learning to Spend from God's Pocket.

No More

DEBT

Credit crunch

CREDIT

recession

Recession

£20

Volume 1

CHARLES OMOLE

AUTHOR: "BREAKING OUT OF DEBT TRAP & PROSPERITY UNLEASHED"

How to ARGUE with God and WIN!

Biblical strategies on getting God's attention for all your circumstances, all of the time.

REV. CHARLES OMOLE

Another Best-seller from Pastor Charles Omole

Printed in Poland
by Amazon Fulfillment
Poland Sp. z o.o., Wrocław